Beautiful Spring! For Kids

Nature Books for Kids
By K. Bennett
Mendon Cottage Books

JD-Biz Publishing

Read More Amazing Animal Books

Purchase at Amazon.com

Download Free Books!
http://MendonCottageBooks.com

Table of Contents

Introduction 4

Spring: 4

Baby animals 5

Baby birds 6

Chapter 1 8

Why do plants love spring? 8

What is composting? 9

Make a garden! 12

Chapter 2 16

Spring is amazing! 16

Chapter 3 24

Seasonal changes: 27

FUN SPRING ACTIVITIES FOR KIDS! 28

Conclusion: 33

Author Bio 36

Publisher 41

Introduction

*Look deep into nature, and then you will understand everything better~ **Albert Einstein***

***

Spring: Spring is a wonderful season with lots of bright colors and warm sunlight! It starts in the month of March.

For three months, planet earth is full of new leaves, beautiful flowers, and lots of new life. The air smells fresh and clean and many children love to play games in the bright green grass. What about you? Do you like to play in the bright green grass?

You might think of spring with the bright sun shining all the time. But spring is not just full of sunshine. There is lots of rain too!

The day might be nice and warm but in some parts of the world at nighttime, it might get a little windy and cool. Rain is very important in springtime. Do you know why?

Rainy days helps plants to grow much better! And when the plants grow better they will have lots of pretty green leaves. The rain also helps other trees to grow big and strong and it helps the flowers stay bright with nice perfume!

Baby animals

Many baby animals are born in spring. One of them is cows. Cows have baby calves during spring and the babies are very happy! Do you know why the baby calves love spring so much?

Because the rain helps the green grass to grow and that is what many animals like to eat, including horses and cows.

Eating good green grass also helps the Mother cow to make good, nutritious milk for her baby. So both mother and baby are very happy!

Baby birds

Baby birds love spring too and many birds build a nest and have their babies during this wonderful season.

One bird that sits on their nest during springtime is called a Cardinal. They usually build their nests during March or April.

A cardinal is a very beautiful bird. Do you know what color they typically are?

Did you guess **red?** Very good!

Some cardinals nest for a long time…all the way in August and even September! But for the most part, during springtime is good for them.

Lots of other birds are the same way. Can you think of any names? If you have an idea, look it up and share your findings with others!

What else happens in the springtime?

Many animals that hibernate (or sleep) during the winter wake up in the springtime!

Frogs also start a family and a frog mother can produce many eggs.

Lots of other activities happen during springtime and many celebrations too. You might know about some of them like: Earth Day, April fool's day, Passover, Cinco de Mayo and more.

Spring is such a happy time! Let's learn more about this beautiful season.

Chapter 1

Learning is fun!

Why do plants love spring?

Spring is a very special time for many plants. You already know that many plants get a lot of new leaves but do you know why?

Plants need special ingredients to grow really well. Do you know what they are?

Did you think of water? Very good!

What about good soil or compost? Do you know what compost is? *Ecofriendlykids.co.uk* helps us to understand what we can do to help our plants to grow.

What is composting?

When we throw away our garbage in the wrong way, it can dirty our beautiful planet. This is called pollution.

Of course we never want to make our planet dirty, so we need to be careful when we throw away our garbage.

And if we put the garbage into the ocean, guess what happens to the beautiful sea life?

You might say it's a good idea to burn it all up! But when we burn our garbage guess where the smoke goes? Did you say: In the air? Yes! You are right. And this type of smoke can pollute our planet too!

This is why composting is a great choice. So let's see what it is all about.

Natural things break down naturally. They get very old after a time and soon they go back into the ground.

This does NOT apply to things like plastic, glass or metal objects. These types of things do not break down well.

The best things to compost are:

-Vegetable Peels

-Grass cuttings

-Leaves

-Flowers

-Fruit Peels

-Egg Shells

-Coffee Grounds

-Bread – stale and things like this…

Remember: It has to be NATURAL.

When you get all these things together, put them in a special place in your yard or garden. It can be a garbage can or just pile them up in a heap.

After a while, it will start to get very old and soon lots of creepy crawlies will take over! Yes, things like wiggly worms. Don't get scared! This has to happen for your compost to work well.

You will know it is ready when your heap looks like crumbled dirt and it smells like the ground. Then you can use it to put around your plants and or mix it in the soil.

What else do plants need?

Did you think of the sun? Wonderful! Yes, plants need the warm sunlight to grow and during spring the sun is nice and strong. And the sun shines for longer hours, which helps the plant to grow much better.

So, plants need these 3 ingredients to grow well:

-Good soil
-Water
-Lots of warm sunlight!

Many people love to plant during springtime. They love the idea of fresh flowers and beautiful plants. The University of Illinois helps us to make a special garden. Maybe you might like to make one too! Here is how you can get started…

Make a garden!

The first thing you need is a great spot! Pick out a really nice place to plant your garden. Make sure it is nice and sunny! If you live in a place with a nice yard it might be easier to make a pretty garden. But even if you live in place with a small yard, you can still make a pretty garden too, only smaller!

What else do you need?

Water! Good water to keep your plants nice and moist. And if your home doesn't have much sunlight, don't worry! There are many plants that grow in the shade! Plants like: Lettuce, begonias, mustard, spinach and many more.

An important step...

Good dirt or soil to help your plant grow. Don't forget what we learned about composting.

Something else to think about:

Plants have roots and the roots go deep into the ground. If water stays on the top of the soil for a long time, will the roots of the plant get the water it needs?

Did you say no? Very good!

Another step is to water your plants the right way. If you give it too little your little plant will die and if you give it too much, your little plant will drown.

So be careful and measure the water you pour on your plants. Your parents can help you or you could research online. Don't forget to get permission before you do!

And the final step is...

FERTILIZER! Plants love nutrients like potassium, nitrogen and phosphorus. Can you guess where to find these nutrients? Yes! You find them in fertilizers. So ask your parents to help you pick out some good fertilizer to help your plants grown healthy and strong.

Isn't this a nice spring project?

(Source: http://extension.illinois.edu/firstgarden/basics/index.cfm)

Chapter 2

Spring is amazing!

There are lots of amazing things that happen during spring. You might notice the sun rising sooner and setting later. And around the world many people celebrate spring in many different ways. Special trees also blossom during springtime.

Have you ever heard of the Cherry Blossom Tree? This tree is very beautiful and when it starts to bloom, spring is near! In our book *"Beautiful Flowers for Kids"* we talked about the Cherry Blossom Tree.

"In the Northern Hemisphere in places like China, Japan, West Siberia, Europe and the United States, there are many beautiful Cherry Blossom trees…One of the best known Cherry blossom species is the Japanese Cherry blossom, also called "Sakura."

Did you know this beautiful tree belongs to the Rose family? Perhaps that is why people love them so much!"

Size: Usually Cherry Blossom trees grow between 25 – 50 feet tall. The canopy (the part of the tree that spreads over the ground) can extend to 40 feet wide but some trees get bigger than that! In their native habitat, this beautiful and exotic tree can grow up to 75 feet.

What a beautiful tree that blooms during spring!

Trees are not the only thing that blossoms during spring. Lots of children blossom too! Did you know that children grow a lot more during spring? What about you? Did you grow a lot in springtime?

There are fun spring activities too!

Here are some ideas for you...

You might like to ride a bicycle through a field of flowers and smell their sweet perfume! Or you might like to walk on a nice trail and take a hike. Which one do you like best? Riding or hiking?

If you don't like these ideas… how about a nice, tasty picnic? You can go to a nice park near your home and enjoy the warm sun with friends and family.

Or you might enjoy a visit to the local farm to see the baby animals! That will be lots of fun and you can learn about them too.

Don't forget to get permission from a parent or guardian before you do anything!

You can even play with your friends or brothers and sisters and there are lots of fun games you can try. Maybe play with your toys or with a ball.

Can you remember the last time you flew a kite?

There are lots of other activities to try during springtime and here is a small list to give you more ideas!

-Go on a treasure hunt

-Ride a gentle horse

-Jump into puddles and have fun squishing the mud through your toes!

-Go to the pond and feed the ducks. See if any baby ducks are born and feed them too!

-Climb a tree and pick some fruit. Be careful when you climb and don't fall!

-Go on a spring vacation with your family!

-Watch the raindrops fall from the sky

-Find a rainbow and count the colors

-Listen to the birds singing beautiful songs

-Go to the zoo and meet the animals

You may have lots more ideas to add to this list, but whatever choice you make don't forget to have fun!

FUN FACTS FOR KIDS:

There are twelve months in a calendar year. Can you guess which months are: Spring, Summer, Autumn and Winter?

Spring: March, April and May

Summer: June, July and August

Autumn: September, October and November

Winter: December, January and February.

Now you know. Don't forget to share what you learn. *Remember:* Sharing is caring!

Chapter 3

Did you have fun learning a little about springtime? Wonderful! Here are just a few more facts you may like to know!

-The first day of spring has a very interesting name. It is called a **VERNAL EQUINOX.** Does that sound strange to you? This word comes from Latin and VERNAL means: Spring. And EQUINOX means: Equal night.

The idea is that the first day of spring should be 12 hour or daylight and 12 hours of night light but this doesn't always happen! Some people who study about this subject say it happens before spring but this gives you an idea where spring got its name!

-We have already talked about the beautiful flowers blooming in spring but there are special flowers that love springtime. Flowers like daffodils, tulips, lilacs, dandelions, lilies and many more! This is what makes spring so beautiful and colorful too.

-Around the world there are very interesting stories about springtime. This one comes from Mexico and place called Chichen Itza. On the first day of spring the Mayan people celebrate "the return of the serpent." Why do they do that? Because in the evening when the sun sets the shadow on the pyramid looks like a snake going down the stairs!

-You probably know about the legend of the groundhog and his shadow! It is said if the groundhog does not see his shadow when he comes out of his burrow, spring will come early.

-In Japan, the opening of the Cherry Blossom says spring is here! The Japanese have a beautiful way of enjoying the Cherry Blossom trees during springtime. Would you like to know what they do?

"The tradition of **Hanami** (Flower viewing) has been celebrated for a very long time... People gather together in groups to watch the beautiful flowers bloom. This can be done during the day or even at night. Beautiful paper lanterns are hung in many areas where the trees are planted (usually a park area), for the guests to enjoy a happy time together. Sometimes the head of a company will send their worker to reserve the best spot in the park. Do you know why? They want their employees to enjoy a "blossomy" evening!"

What about you? Do you have any special way to enjoy the flowers and trees?

-Honeybees are very active during springtime and form new colonies. The funny thing is that during springtime, honeybees are very friendly!

-Remember that during springtime it can be windy too! In the United States, Tornadoes are very active during springtime.

-Some places do not have spring. Places around the equator have the same season all year round. The weather there is usually nice, warm and sunny all the time! Other places have seasonal changes and can be dry or wet! Do you remember what Seasonal changes means?

Seasonal changes: Natural changes that happen during spring, summer, autumn and winter. Remember what happens during spring? New leaves start to grow, flowers blossom and the air is fresh and clean!

-Monarch butterflies are very active during spring. They lay their tiny eggs on milkweed plants and soon beautiful butterflies are flying in the air!

-Hummingbirds have a lot of fun during springtime too! Males have fun performing amazing acrobatics to impress the females.

Lots of exciting things happen during springtime!

FUN SPRING ACTIVITIES FOR KIDS!

There are lots of fun craft activities online with amazing spring projects! Here are two you might like to try. They are adapted from *Choices4children.blogspot.com*

Are you ready? Then let's get started.

For this project you will need the following items:

-Paper

-Stencils

-Crayons

-Liquid water colors

-Spray bottles

This project is very simple and easy to do. Just place the stencil over the paper, spray your liquid water color and watch a work of art come to life! When you are done, you can use the crayons to give more color or depth to your beautiful picture. Use different shapes for more variety. Very good!

Housingaforest.com has another cute project to make a spring cheery tree painting! This is what you will need:

-Watercolor paper

-Watercolors, brushes and a container of water to clean them.

-Black acrylic paint. You will have to add water to make the paint thinner.

-Straw

-Eye dropper

-Shades of pink, white and purple acrylic paint.

Before you get started, here is a great tip at the website: wet your paper for the color to blend better! Your brush should also be wet before you dip it into the paint. A spray bottle will help to keep rewetting the paper if needed.

Start with the grass and the sky. Use different shades of color to make it really nice. After you have your grass and the sky just the way you want it, put it aside and let it dry.

When it is dry you are ready to add your tree. Remember that your black paint should be watery. So add water to make it really thin. Take your eye dropper and add a drop of black paint.

Use a straw and blow…don't blow too hard…just blow gently so your little drop of paint can spread across the paper.

Make the base and trunk of the tree. Blow down to create it. Then angle your straw to blow up and across to make the branches. If you are not sure how it will work, you might practice this part first!

Once you have the shape of a tree with lots of dark branches set it aside to dry.

Now let's add the blossoms!

Blend the shades to get the precise color you want. Once you blend the colors enough, use your fingers to dab on the branches until the tree is covered in beautiful cherry blossoms. Great job!

I hope you enjoy these projects and don't forget to have fun!

KEEP LEARNING!

Spring is one of the four seasons. And the reason why we have seasons is because of the earth's tilt towards the sun. Do you remember how many degrees it is tilted? Can you guess?

1- **14.76°**

2- **20.22°**

3- **23.45°**

If you choose number 3 you are correct! This is what gives the earth the beautiful seasons during the year.

And during the spring season you will hear many different words that people use during springtime. Words like:

-Blooms
-Spring Break
-Spring Cleaning

-Snowdrop

-Easter eggs

-Foal

-Galoshes

-Crocus

-Bulbs

-Bud

-Kid (Clue: it is not a person but an animal.)

-Rebirth

-Slicker

-Vernal equinox

Do you know what these words mean? If you are not sure, ask your parent or a guardian's permission to help you find the definition. Hope you learn something new!

Conclusion:

In conclusion: Spring, like each of the four seasons, is unique and does wonderful things for our planet. Would you like to continue learning about this beautiful season?

Ideas to help you!

Why don't you research how some animals wake up during springtine? If you don't know which animals hibernate during spring, here is a small list to get started.

-The alpine marmot.

-Black Bears

-Eastern Chipmunks

-Eastern Box turtle

-Bats

-Ladybugs and many more!

Maybe you know of other creatures that hibernate during winter too. Can you share your ideas with others?

Think of show and tell at school or another school project. Can you talk about spring and share with your teacher and classmates? Maybe you can tell them why you like it so much and what makes it different from other seasons!

Maybe you could use the *Spring Cleaning* idea for show and tell. For this project you will need to have a broom, a mop, empty pails, some cleaning rags, spray bottles, and more. Then you could show what each item is for and how it can help you to spring clean in the best way!

How about a nice nature walk? On your walk, why don't you find new plants that just started to grow? Can you see new butterflies flying around? What about birds? Do you hear new sounds you haven't heard before?

You might decide to adopt a tree! Take a picture of a small tree and keep a chart on it for a few months or a year. When spring comes around again, did the tree grow a lot or not very much?

(Source: http://stepbystepcc.com/spring3.html)

Just one more!

What about the Ocean? Does anything special happen during springtime? Did you know the ocean blooms? But how does it bloom?

This amazing process is called the North Atlantic Bloom and it happens when sunlight mixes with Carbon Dioxide and the phytoplankton in the sea start to grow!

As you can see there are lots of things we can learn about this amazing season.

If you don't like the ideas in this book, put on your thinking cap and come up with your own conclusions!

I hope you have enjoyed this book on Beautiful Spring. And remember...

 *"Educating the mind without educating the heart is no education at all."* - *Aristotle*

Author Bio

K. Bennett loves to write for both children and adults. Many different subjects are interesting to develop, but writing for children is special to her heart.

Her favorite pastimes include reading, traveling and discovering new things. Each of these activities helps to fuel her imagination and acts like a blank canvas waiting for more stories.

She is intrigued with fantasy elements like hidden worlds and faraway lands. And basically anything that gets her imagination soaring to new heights!

Her writing credits include children books online, short stories for online magazines, and novellas listed at Amazon.com

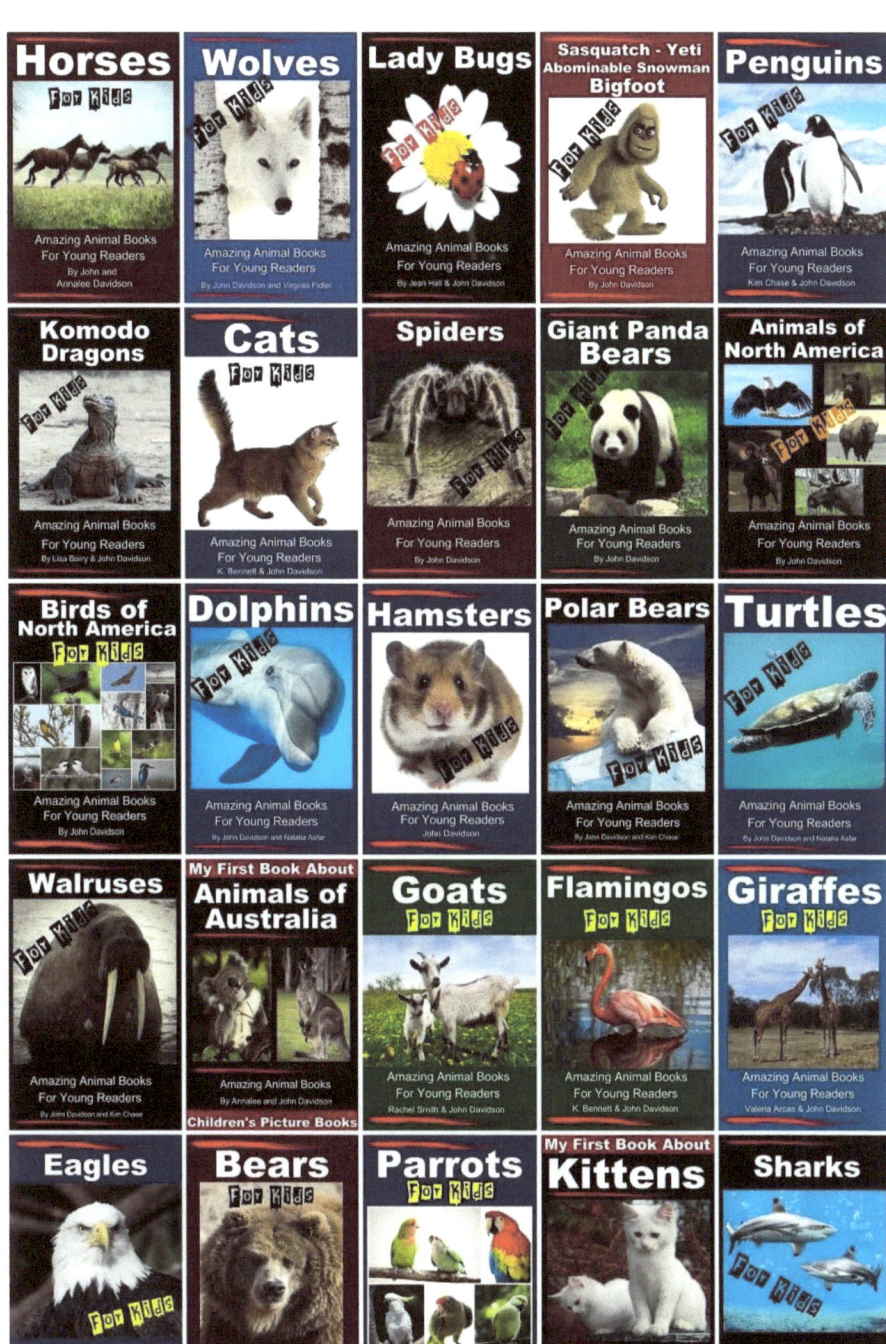

Our books are available at

1. Amazon.com

2. Barnes and Noble

3. Itunes

4. Kobo

5. Smashwords

6. Google Play Books

Download Free Books!
http://MendonCottageBooks.com

Publisher

JD-Biz Corp

P O Box 374

Mendon, Utah 84325

http://www.jd-biz.com/

www.ingramcontent.com/pod-product-compliance
Lightning Source LLC
Chambersburg PA
CBHW050847290526
45792CB00002B/559